to Fern
with Love

Stuart + Isabella.

LUMBER CAMP
LIFE
in Michigan

An Autobiographical Account by
Jacob Dye—1880-1893
and His Son
Rex J. Dye—1904-1909

An Exposition-Lochinvar Book

Exposition Press   *Hicksville, New York*

Contents

PREFACE   5

AUTOBIOGRAPHY OF JACOB DYE FROM 1880 to 1893   9

1904-1909:   RECOLLECTIONS OF REX DYE, SON OF JACOB DYE   21

LOCALITIES
MENTIONED
IN THE TEXT

MECOSTA—Jacob Dye was born in Sheridan Township, Mecosta County, Michigan, in 1875. Mecosta was then a lumbering town and camps were in the area.

SHARON—a lumbering town with tie camps in the area. Rex J. Dye and his brother, Leland, walked to school here from camps about three-miles distant.

NAPLES—a tent "city" of huckleberry pickers in 1905.

SIGMA—a lumbering town a few miles north of Sharon.

KALKASKA—Rex J. Dye and his brother attended school here.

TRAVERSE CITY—Logs were floated down the Boardman River to this city from the Kalkaska-Sigma area.

BOYNE FALLS—Jacob Dye had camps in this area. Rex J. Dye was born in a lumber camp here.

BOYNE CITY—Tan bark was loaded on sailing vessels here.

HUBBEL JUNCTION (now Rexton)—Jacob Dye worked in a camp four miles from here in 1892.

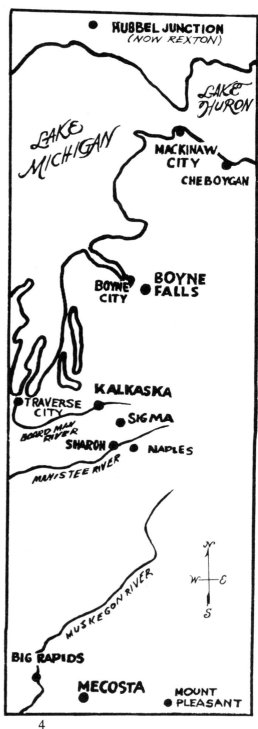

4

Preface

This little book has been prepared for the purpose of recording a firsthand, eyewitness account of life, activities and environment of the early days of Michigan lumber camps. It is not a history of Michigan lumbering, but only a glimpse of some aspects of that history. The period covered herein started ninety-four years ago and ended seventeen years later. The social, economic, and industrial changes since this brief period, which ended only sixty-seven years ago, have been so drastic and far-reaching as to make this record seem of the far-distant past! I am wondering what the ways of life of 1974 will look like to those living in the year 2011, only sixty-seven years away!

The photographs herein were from a collection my father had saved. Many photographs from this collection were lost. He hired photographers such as D. E. Whipple of Fife Lake and a man named Beebe to come to his camp and photograph activities.

LUMBER CAMP
LIFE
in Michigan

Jacob Dye—1880-1893

Jacob Dye when twenty-one years old. This photo, taken in 1896, shows a double-bitted axe with a curved handle, apparently a photographer's "prop," as it would be impossible to use the double-bitted axe with such a handle, a straight handle being always used with this axe.

Jacob Dye at age eighty-four. This photo was taken, developed and printed by Rex J. Dye. It is an excellent likeness. He died September 26, 1961, at the age of eighty-six at Novi, Michigan.

Autobiography of Jacob Dye from 1880 to 1893

Written by Jacob Dye at Age Eighty-Four

I was born in 1875 in Sheridan Township, Mecosta County, Michigan.

I will always remember that big hill up which we carried water! Sometimes Dad (Morris G. Dye) would draw a barrelful up with the oxen which saved lots of steps for my brothers and me. I remember in 1880 and 1881, during the open winter that was so bad for the lumberman, there was no snow to haul logs to the river and most every lumberman went broke.

The large pine trees on my father's homestead are also fresh in my memory for the following reason. Father came from Ohio and did not know how long pine stumps would last and that they would not rot like hardwood. He girdled the pines so they would die and rot away so he could clear and farm the land, which was the main idea in his mind at that time. They did not rot and gave him a lot of work clearing.

Above: Birthplace of Rex J. Dye, a lumber camp near Boyne Falls, Michigan, one of the earliest camps Jacob Dye owned. From right, unidentified; Jacob Dye; Grace Dye; her mother, Mary Sullivan.

Below: Scene in front of camp buildings, 1898. Morris Dye, father of Jacob, second from right.

During the winter of 1881 and 1882 there was a school-house built on the southwest corner of father's homestead. It was built of hemlock logs about twenty feet wide with a flat roof made of logs split in half and then troughed out like eaves. These troughed-out logs were placed so the troughs were up on the bottom layer with the overlapping troughs down on the top layer, making a roof which did not let the water in or keep the wind out.

My father was the teacher the first school year which was four months long. Three brothers and a sister from one other family, myself, and three of my brothers were the only students that first year. The second year a new family came into the area with two more children and we had two terms of three months each.

We were getting too big for the old schoolhouse and the school board voted to build a nice frame school building one-half mile south of the old school, with about one acre of land for the school lot. It was right in the woods with virgin timber on all four sides. We spent a lot of happy days here. I drove past this spot in 1927 and stopped, looking back and thinking what a change had taken place in forty years!

About 1885 our house, built of hewed logs, burned down, a sight I will always remember. It was a total loss. By this time there were nine children in our family. Father and Mother were so grieved they gave up the farm and moved to Mecosta, then a small lumbering town where I saw, for the first time, a railroad train.

I was now about fourteen years old with three brothers older than myself. We all worked and got a home started. We made friends fast and really lived for a few years. Then came the panic of 1893 with hard times for nearly everybody. The family began to get separated, one brother in Wisconsin, another in North Dakota.

Above: Railroad ties ready to be hauled to railroad for shipment. Jacob Dye, center of three men standing.

Skidding crew with logs to be hauled to skidways for "decking" in piles.

When I was fifteen years old, my oldest brother came home and wanted me to go with him to saw logs for the George Collins Lumber Company at a camp ten miles north of Horsehead Lake.

Father and Mother agreed to this. I walked the fifteen miles to the camp on a Sunday afternoon and became a real lumberjack and the youngest man on the company time book.

My brother and I had the job of sawing logs for what was called the bucking crew. Each crew had six men and two horses. Their job was to cut, skin, and deck logs for sleigh hauling.

A timber fitter planned the falling of the trees so that they could be sawed into logs as easily as possible. He determined the proper length to cut the logs, so that when they were cut into lumber, they would produce the most profit. He also planned the falling of trees so brush and waste parts would be out of the way when it came to skidding the logs.

Two swampers cut and piled brush out of the way, so the logs could be dragged on the ground by a team of horses to the skidways for decking. Logs were often decked fifteen to twenty feet high in large piles.

Our crews were not known by a man's name, but instead were identified by the names of horses and teamsters of each crew. Our crew was Fred and Prince Collins.

The logs were scaled each day which gave the information on how much timber they contained. The total for each crew for the day was posted each evening on a "bucking" board. Every man was interested in making as good a showing as possible. The amount of logs sawed, skidded, and decked by each team was generally about the same.

This camp had twelve teams skidding or twelve crews

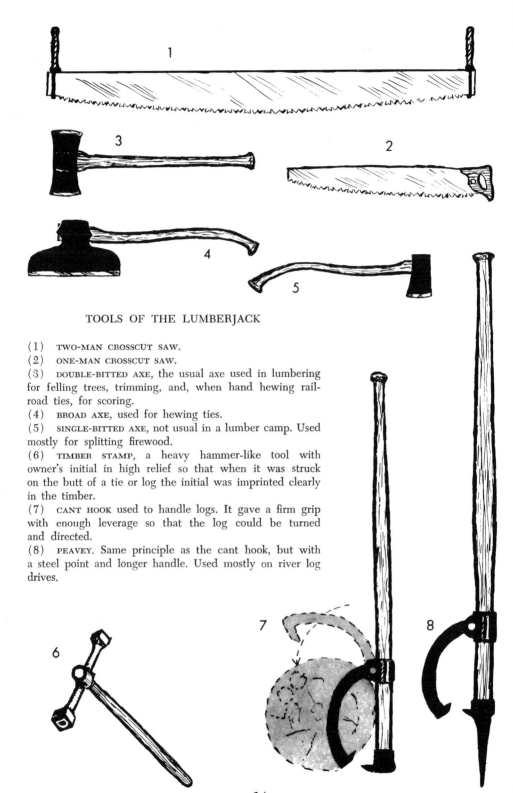

TOOLS OF THE LUMBERJACK

(1) TWO-MAN CROSSCUT SAW.

(2) ONE-MAN CROSSCUT SAW.

(3) DOUBLE-BITTED AXE, the usual axe used in lumbering for felling trees, trimming, and, when hand hewing railroad ties, for scoring.

(4) BROAD AXE, used for hewing ties.

(5) SINGLE-BITTED AXE, not usual in a lumber camp. Used mostly for splitting firewood.

(6) TIMBER STAMP, a heavy hammer-like tool with owner's initial in high relief so that when it was struck on the butt of a tie or log the initial was imprinted clearly in the timber.

(7) CANT HOOK used to handle logs. It gave a firm grip with enough leverage so that the log could be turned and directed.

(8) PEAVEY. Same principle as the cant hook, but with a steel point and longer handle. Used mostly on river log drives.

14

of six men, and one team of horses doing the foregoing work. At the end of each week, the crew having the biggest scale of logs received a premium of fifty cents apiece in trade at the camp store for clothing, mittens, tobacco, and such.

The buildings in the camps where we stayed were built about eighty feet long, about eight feet high at the wall, and about twenty-four feet wide with a peaked roof. This pitched roof made the ceiling high which helped the ventilation of this large room where from one hundred to one hundred thirty men slept in bunks. These bunks were like a box about four feet wide, six feet long, and about eight inches deep, filled with straw. Each man had two heavy blankets and if you could get a grain sack to fill with straw you had a pillow. If you couldn't get a grain sack, you just did the best you could without one.

But the food was good and lots of it. The dining room had three tables each about forty feet long with benches on both sides. Every man had his own place at the table and not a word was spoken at the meal, except to have something passed to you that you could not reach, which was seldom. A man could be discharged quicker for any disorder in the dining room than for almost anything else.

GRINDSTONE. This was turned by hand by one man while another ground the axe. A water can with a hole in it dripped water on the stone. After grinding, the lumberjack would use a whetstone to get a razor-sharp edge.

Top: Jacob on load of logs to be hauled to mill on sleighs.

The second picture shows him ready to "take off" and the bottom picture shows him going down the iced road with coattails flying! Logs were securely fastened to the sleighs with heavy chains. Roads were iced by going over them with a water sprinkler on a sleigh. After freezing, the road was slippery enough to make hauling possible.

At 9:00 P.M. sharp lights were put out by the chore boy who had full charge. Everything had to be quiet till 5:00 A.M. when the cook blew the horn for us to get ready for breakfast. At 5:30 A.M. he blew the horn again to come and eat it.

About the middle of January I got tired of the camp and went home. I got a due bill for the balance due me and got some groceries for my folks at home. I was proud of what I had earned and it helped the family a lot.

By spring I was anxious to go someplace again and so started searching for work. I finally got a job sorting lumber and it was hard work. While the foreman was very good to me, it was too hard for me and I had to give it up, although it paid $1.35 per day for only eleven hours work with 57¢ a day taken off for board, which was good pay at that time.

I rested up at home for awhile and had lots of fun with my brothers and sisters for a few weeks. I then heard that the railroad from Mecosta to Winchester and on to Barrington was started. I got a job from a good old Irishman named John Doyle as a handy boy on the construction, and worked at this job for about three months. I found I could get better pay than the railroad could give me out in the timber, where ties were being made for the railroad; so I quit my friend, Mr. Doyle. I went to work scoring ties for Dad Evens, a grand old man who would only hire young fellows. He paid $1.50 a day and board with pay every week.

I now had lots of money and lots of fun. I chewed tobacco, smoked Peerless, and took a drink now and then. I felt I was a grown man now!

By the end of summer the railroad had gotten to Winchester and stopped for the winter. I went back home and there was not much work to be had. A man around Mecosta was getting woodsmen together for work in the upper pen-

insula so I took a job with him. We shipped in November
to Hubbel Junction on the Soo Line which is where Rexton
is now. The camp was four miles from Hubbel Junction.
All we could do here was work, but we were happy. We
had stag dances, played cards, and got along well. In April
of 1893 I left to get out of the snow and headed for home.
(Jacob Dye was eighteen years of age at the time this
narrative ends.)

Jacob Dye continued in the lumbering business and
being an aggressive, driving man, established himself as an
owner. He was able to do any job in lumbering, including
scaling logs, timber cruising, and selling the product.

On July 2, 1898, he married Gracie Sullivan and on
September 12, 1899, a son, Rex J. Dye, was born. No record
exists for the years intervening between 1893 and 1898, but
by the time his first son was born, he was twenty-four years
old and he had his own camp.

He operated in the Boyne Falls-Sharon-Sigma area,
largely in cedar which included railroad ties (hand hewed
and later sawed by mill), fence posts, shingles and floats
for commercial fishing nets. He did some lumbering in
hardwood and pine but cedar was the primary wood. He
later worked as a tie inspector and buyer for the Pierre
Marquette Railroad.

LUMBER CAMP
LIFE
in Michigan

Rex J. Dye—1904-1909

A typical oxen team. The young man in the background is Rex J. Dye.

Rex J. Dye and his brother, Leland, having a "swim" in Cannon Creek. (It makes me shiver to look at this photo now as those streams never got much above freezing!)

1904-1909: Recollections of Rex Dye, son of Jacob Dye

I was born in one of the first of my father's lumber camps near Boyne Falls, Michigan, in 1899. Many of my recollections of the lumbering days are like still pictures taken from a single frame of movie film with no memory of preceding or subsequent frames or events, and with no remembrances of their sequence. Memory is an interesting phenomenon. Perhaps the introduction of an experience removed from the usual routine of activity, and so possessing unique characteristics, makes a much stronger impression on one's consciousness than ordinary day-to-day occurrences and so accounts for this retention in memory. Such experiences gain high attention values, particularly where they are pleasurable.

Among the earliest of such remembered events is that of sitting astride my father's back, legs on each side of his neck, while he was "timber cruising." Timber cruising was a matter of checking out a stand of timberland to determine what it would yield as a logging operation.

The method employed three men, one to the right and one to the left of the timber cruiser. They would start at

Scene on the river at Central Lake, Michigan, about 1906. Peaveys were used in this work, as well as long poles to keep the floating logs moving.

Logs were floated by river to Manistee down the Manistee River from the Sharon-Sigma area and down the Boardman River to Traverse City. They were hauled to locations along the rivers and slid into the water at steep banks or chutes. Men followed the logs and their destination on rafts. When the logs jammed and stopped moving, men went out on the jam with peaveys and poles and got them moving again.

Below: Millpond at the Wells-Higman Co. on the Boardman River at Traverse City.

one side of the wooded tract, one man at the west boundary, some distance farther into the woods would be the cruiser, and about the same distance farther into the woods would be the third man of the team. Starting at the boundary, for example the north limit of the woods, they would walk south guided by compass until they reached the southern boundary. Then the cruiser would move to the east of the man on his left, who would work back along the same path he first took south, and the man on his right would shift to the east of the timber cruiser. Then the group would go north to the northern boundary. In this manner, maintaining about the same distances between each man, they would traverse the entire tract. When the tract was covered the timber cruiser would know with surprising accuracy what the tract would yield in terms of board feet when the logging crews went through it. I have no idea how this estimate was arrived at. I only recall the memory of going through the woods in this manner and my father telling me what they were doing. I do not remember where we came from nor where we went afterwards, but this recollection is vivid. I have the compass he used. It is set in two solid hinged pieces of mahogany about 3½" square which close like a box and deactivate the compass needle.

Another scene that occurs to me while with my father was seeing an old small locomotive rusted and alone on a short piece of track surrounded by second growth timber. It was a woodburner and had a funnel shaped smokestack. The rails stopped at each end of the engine. No track led away from it. It had apparently been abandoned while the rails it had once steamed over had been pulled up and taken away. New growth had obliterated the roadbed it had once traveled. I have often wondered who used this engine and what has happened to it since I saw it. I do not re-

Above: Loading logs on flatcars at Sigma, Michigan, about 1910. Note the "boom" with man standing on log in air. Logs were raised with this "boom" and jockeyed into position by a man with a cant hook. Man in light coat is holding a cant hook.

Below: E&M Steamhauler, Black River, Sheboygan County, Michigan. A real early caterpillar! About 1907.

member where it was nor anything of the day before or the day after. I was probably about five years old at the time.

Another early recollection is being on a large raft which had a tent on it and a small iron stove. It was afloat on a river behind a lot of logs, which were probably being floated to some millpond farther downstream. In connection with this, I can remember logs shooting down from the river bank into the river, making a big splash as they hit the water, but here again no preceeding or subsequent events come to mind.

Again, I remember riding in the caboose of a train. I was sitting in the little cupola at the top of the caboose . . . and my straw hat blew out the window. The conductor pulled a cord of some kind and stopped the train and after they told the engineer what had happened, the train backed up and they got my hat! Where we came from or where we were going I do not remember, but this incident is still vivid in my memory.

I can also remember being in a rowboat on a millpond with a lot of logs around us. Why we were there I do not know, but I suppose it was for some kind of checkup on the logs which had been floated down the river to the mill. The fact that being in a boat was a new and unusual experience for me perhaps accounts for the fact that this experience is remembered.

My first memories of my father's lumber camps include the way they were built, the daily routine involved, the discipline my father maintained, and the activities of lumberjacks in the camps, in the woods, and in town on pay days.

I recall living in a log building at one time but the camp buildings I remember most clearly were of rough sawed

Logs at mill yard ready to be processed into lumber, railroad ties, shingles, and floats for commercial fishing nets.

Building a lumber mill in the timber country was quite an operation in itself in the early 1900s. I recall my father doing this. He wanted his mill located near the source of raw material and so got a better price for mill products than for logs and cut hauling costs. He had to build a road in order to get the steam engine, saw mill, and equipment to the mill site. The road was used later to haul lumber, railroad ties, shingles, and fishermen's floats to the rail shipping point.

Kerosene lamps and lanterns were the lighting equipment used in the camps. The wall lamp with a slot in the hanger to fit over a nail in the wall was generally used in the buildings.

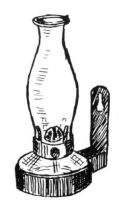

lumber covered with tar paper. The camp included a men shanty, a cook shanty, and a blacksmith shop, as well as stables for the horses. Later camps had a sawmill for cutting railroad ties which replaced the hewed tie. Additional equipment for cutting lumber, making shingles, and later floats for commercial fishing nets were added. These machines were powered with a wood-burning steam engine and all this equipment was hauled through the timber to the camp location with teams of horses. A lot of clearing and road building was necessary to get this machinery through the woods to the site where it was to be in operation.

The cook shanty had a kitchen and a dining room which was furnished with long tables and benches made on the spot. The men shanty had rows of bunks along the walls for sleeping. These bunks were equipped with mattresses and springs and were double decked like those in a sleeping car. My father believed he could get better men and more work done if he offered good beds and good food. These were what we might call today "fringe benefits" that would be found in few lumber camps at that time. Perhaps his previous experience with camp food and straw "mattresses" led him to take this view.

The blacksmith shop had a forge which was operated with a hand bellows, an anvil, hammers and tongs of various kinds, a vise, files and other tools for repairing equipment, sharpening saws, and making various things.

Horse barns had stalls for horses and storage areas for hay and grain, as well as racks for harness, log chains, and other equipment.

Outhouses were rough shacks with a long pole from which the bark had been removed with a drawknife for a seat, strategically placed parallel to the pit, not the last word in comfort, but practical.

These various buildings were usually covered with tar

Above: Stove wood was an important commodity in the early days. This photo shows several carloads of chunk wood split to stove length ready for shipment.

Below: Front Street in Traverse City in 1906. There was quite a lot of commercial fishing here, and Jacob Dye manufactured cedar floats for nets and sold them to these fishermen.

paper to keep out rain and melted snow and were heated by wood-burning stoves made of sheet iron.

The daily routine at the camps was basically rise at dawn and work till night. After breakfast the timber crews left for the locations they were working in, taking a substantial supply of food with them for the noon meal. Upon returning to camp at the end of the day they cleaned up and had a hearty supper following which they busied themselves with such chores as sharpening axes, filing saws, sawing up firewood, greasing their boots, and similar jobs.

Axes were sharpened on a hand turned grindstone which had a can of water rigged over the top of the circular stone from which water ran in a very small stream to the face of the stone. The axe was held to this face and ground to the highest sharpness the stone could produce, after which the lumberjack went to work on the cutting edge of the axe with a whetstone, producing a razor sharp edge.

Grindstones were made at Grindstone City, a community at the tip of the "thumb" between Huron City and Point Au Barques, Michigan. Grindstones were shipped by water to many industrial areas. Grindstone City had quarries where huge deposits of sandstone suitable for this use made this industry possible. The harbor here is still bordered with hundreds of rejected grindstones used as breakwaters. Some of these stones are several feet in diameter.

I remember turning grindstones for the lumberjacks and when they wanted to horseplay, they would bear down heavily with the axe on the stone which made it hard to turn. Then they would ease up and laugh about it.

Filing saws was a more technical operation which was done by only a few of the men, including my father. The crosscut saws had two cutting teeth beveled to cut each side of the saw path. These two cutting teeth were followed by a "raker" which carried the wood freed by the cutting

Above: Kalkaska was a thriving town in the early 1900s. My brother and I went to school here several winters while our father ran his camp.

Below: My mother, brother, and I watched this fire from a point near the railroad tracks shown previously.

teeth out of the log. The teeth of the saw were filed sharp and the width of the cut by the cutting teeth was set according to the kind of timber on which the saw was used. Saw filing to get the best action from the saw was an art in itself.

Boots were waterproofed by rubbing them with a hot mixture of tallow, beeswax and a little lampblack which they called "lickdob." This mixture was prepared in a large can and heated on one of the stoves in the men shanty. It was applied to the boots with a stick which had cloth wrapped around one end to carry the waterproofing mixture while hot.

The boots they wore were of leather with thick leather soles. The soles were studded with pointed calks which made it possible for the lumberman to work on a fallen tree, trimming, scoring, and hewing it for railroad ties without losing his footing or slipping. When handling a double-bitted axe or a broadaxe standing on the tree you were working on, a slip of the foot could be disastrous. I recall one instance where this happened with the broadaxe blade going through a man's boot, costing him several toes.

Clothing worn by lumberjacks during the winter lumbering operations consisted of "long johns," heavy wool pants which were usually "stagged" (bottom of legs cut off to clear boots), wool shirts, mackinaw-type coats, wool socks, calked boots, and stocking caps or visored wool caps with ear laps.

Work in the woods necessitated clearing roadways and sometimes building roads up with brush trimmed from fallen timber. Sometimes "corduroy" roads were built using small logs laid crossways on the road to provide support for the loads to be hauled.

Logs were loaded on bobsleighs by means of a boom carrying a pulley arrangement with horses supplying the power. One man stood on the sleigh with a cant hook and

Above: My brother and I went to school at this schoolhouse in Sharon, Michigan. We walked three miles from the camp to school.

Below: E. F. Tidd had a grocery and general store in Sharon. Note the depot, a boxcar set on a cedar-post foundation, a quite common practice in small communities then.

guided the logs into position. The logs loaded on the sleigh were held in position by heavy log chains and then hauled to the mill for sawing into railroad ties, shingles, and any needed lumber. Flatcars at rail loading points were also loaded in the same manner as the sleighs.

Logs were scaled with a rule which made it possible to hold the scale in position across the diameter of the butt of the log so the number of board feet could be read.

Roads were kept clear with horse-drawn snowplows and iced over by hauling a water tank with a spray arrangement over the road. This icing served to firm the road and reduce friction for the loads of logs hauled. Skidways to haul logs from the woods to the loading point were also sometimes iced in this manner. Logs were skidded to these points by horses without sleighs; they were simply dragged over the snow.

My father maintained a strict discipline in his camps. He allowed no drinking or card playing and enforced his rules physically when necessary. I recall one incident very clearly which illustrates the type of enforcement he used. He was making the rounds of the camp and I was tagging along behind him. He had hired two new men that day and he might have been checking up on them. He opened the door of the men shanty and walked in. A card game was in progress, apparently started by these two new men. He walked over to the table, grabbed one of them by the front of his shirt, and literally threw him across the room. This one landed in one of the bunks . . . and stayed there. The other fellow, who looked bigger than my father, had gotten up from the table and was ready to start fighting, but he started much too late as my father moved in fast, hit him, and he "went to sleep" on the floor. My father did not fire these men and they were working the next day, but there were no more card games started.

During the summer season when cedar swamps could not be worked, my father operated a huckleberry buying and grocery store at Naples, Michigan, a few miles east of Sharon. The boy with the holster is Rex J. Dye (upper photo). Mother, father, and brother stand in front in lower photo. (Note coffee grinder.)

Huckleberry picker.

Huckleberry picking at Naples was a "big business" in those days. Hundreds of people came here, pitched their tents and picked huckleberries. They sold them to buyers here who shipped them to markets. They used pickers as illustrated, sweeping them over the plants and gathering the berries fast. The tines on the front were of heavy spring steel wire and would separate the berries from the vines so they would roll back into the box of the picker.

This all seems rather brutal, but in those days in that area you couldn't call a policeman, and "law and order" was a matter of a man's will and ability to enforce it. Card games were always for money and could be depended upon to cause serious trouble as was the case with drinking. My father was far from a teetotaler and did not care what these lumberjacks did in town on pay days. If they were drunk they were piled on a sleigh and hauled back to camp after their spree in town, but in the camp drinking was simply not allowed.

Among the tools a lumberjack used were a double-bitted axe with a straight handle, which was an axe with two cutting edges, one used mostly for trimming branches from fallen trees and one used for scoring ties (of which more will be told later); the crosscut saw which came in two basic forms, the one-man saw with a handle similar to a handsaw and the two-man saw, which had an upright round handle at each end which a man could grasp with both hands in order to pull the saw back to himself after his partner had pulled it away from him.

For hewing ties a broadaxe was used. This axe had a heavy blade a foot or more long with a beveled edge like a carpenter's chisel. The handle was curved and it seems to me to have been one of the most ungainly and awkward tools I've ever seen. In the hands of a real tie maker, however, the broadaxe was a beautiful tool. He could produce a finished tie with clean, graceful strokes of this tool with an even thickness and a smooth, true surface. Ties were stamped with a hammerlike tool that left an identifying initial when the butt end of the tie was struck with it.

In handling logs, rolling them into position for cutting, loading on sleighs, and stacking, a cant hook was used. This was a heavy hook type of tool with the hook hinged to a ring through which a rugged, straight handle projected,

Here are two photos of other berry buyers at Naples. The man standing in the top photo is apparently interested in other activities than berry buying as he has a fly rod in his hand and a fishing creel over his shoulder!

terminating in a steel ring with projections at the end which lined up with the point of the swinging hook. As the hook of the tool was free to move to fit various diameters of logs and bite into the log's surface, the cant hook gave a great leverage to the operation of rolling a log or controlling its movements.

A peavey, used mostly for handling logs on the river, was about the same as a cant hook, but the handle extended farther below the hook and carried a heavy spikelike terminal which would not slip when jammed into a log to move it.

Tapelines were used for measuring. Those, I remember, were in a heavy leather case with reel-type action to wind the tape back after using. Drawknives were used for peeling smaller cedar logs for fence posts.

While my father lumbered in hardwood as well as cedar, the cedar camps stand out much stronger in my memory, particularly the tie camps. Cedar was probably the most suitable and longest-lasting timber for railroad ties, and they were much in demand at that time. The first ties I saw made were hewed by hand. Suitable cedar trees were fallen by the lumberjacks, using axes and crosscut saws. These trees were trimmed of all branches and then fixed in position for hewing, supported by logs with an axe driven in on each side of the log to be hewed to insure the stability of the position. The hewing process consisted of two operations: first, scoring with the double-bitted axe by making slanted cuts into the log on each side; second, hewing these two sides to a relatively smooth surface by using the broadaxe with its chisel-shaped cutting edge in long, sweeping strokes in the opposite direction from which the scoring cuts were made. The hewed log was then cut by a crosscut saw to the required lengths for railroad ties and the finished ties were piled for hauling and delivery to rail facilities.

These two photos give some idea of the cedar woods. In streams like Devil Creek you could get nice mess of speckled brook trout easily—if you could get to the water.

After my father acquired his sawmill the hand hewing of railroad ties stopped. Cedar logs were hauled to the mill and there sawed to the required thickness and length. I believe, however, the hewed ties were considered superior to those mill sawed, having a smoother surface which contributed to longer life. Later, I believe, various hardwoods were used with finished ties, being treated with creosote under pressure, perhaps because the supply of cedar had become exhausted.

Two other operations added to the sawmill fascinated me, the first being the shingle mill and the second the making of floats for use by Great Lakes commercial fishermen on their nets.

The shingle mill as I remember it consisted of four fundamental operations: *first*, cutting the logs into sections the proper length for shingles; *second*, sawing to get the wedge shape of the shingle; *third*, knot sawing to get straight and knot free edges, and, *fourth*, to sort, band, and bale.

After the logs were cut into sections of the desired length they were moved to the shingle saw. This was a large circular saw lying flat in a horizontal position, equipped with a tilting movable table that made it possible to cut each successive "slice" from the sections fed into it at the proper angle for use as a shingle. These rough shingles were thrown into a bin for the knot sawyers to cut and trim to finished sizes. The knot saw was a small, high speed circular saw, past which a sliding table was moved by hand carrying the rough cut shingle stock. The knot sawyer placed a piece of the rough cut stock on this table and trimmed it on both sides to what in his judgment was the best width. He then tossed this finished shingle over to the bin behind him for the sorting and baling operation. These high speed knot saws and the sliding table

These two photos show the wild, natural beauty of the area around Sharon, Michigan, at the start of the nineteenth century. Deer were plentiful, bobcats, bear, and fox were common, and rabbits were everywhere. Few men around the lumber camps bothered to hunt.

arrangement were dangerous and many knot sawyers were lacking one or more fingers.

The baling operations consisted of sorting the shingles, no two of which were likely to be of the same width, in successive layers to make up a bundle, then compressing them in a press and fastening them with metal straps to make up a bundle. As these bundles had to be fairly uniform in size and the edges or sides neat and even, this operation must have required a certain talent, especially when working at high speed as these fellows did.

My father, after checking with commercial fishermen at Traverse City, decided to make floats for use on the nets used by this industry on the Great Lakes. These floats were perhaps eight or nine inches long, three inches in diameter, and were rounded on both ends. They had a hole running through the center so they could be threaded on the nets at required intervals. I went to Traverse City once with my father and had a ride on one of the fishing boats, the owner of which used the floats made at the mill of the lumber camp.

Hemlock logs were peeled for the bark to be used in tanning leather. I remember seeing tan bark loaded on big schooners at Boyne City. The loaders were called "dock wallopers." They wore heavy leather aprons and carried the bundles of bark over a gangplank and onto the ship.

The crew of lumberjacks got paid once a month and on pay day they went into town on bobsleighs covered with straw and with a few blankets spread over the straw. Sharon, Michigan, is the town I remember in this connection.

Sharon had a grocery store run by a man named Tidd. He was also an artist and I recall the time he showed me a big artist's palette which he had. Sharon also had, as I recall, two or three saloons, a schoolhouse where I and my brother went to school, a railroad station consisting of a boxcar supported by round cedar blocks, and a few shanties

CITY OF BOYNE.

This little steamboat sailed on Lake Charlevoix between Boyne City and Charlevoix in the early 1900s. I used to delight in standing at the prow near the flag, particularly in stormy weather.

My uncle, Herb Sutton, with a load of lumber. Note the improvised spring seat.

of rough lumber covered with tar paper against the weather. There were no churches in Sharon as I remember it. It was a small "end of the line" community serving the lumbering operations. In the summertime it was a shipping point for huckleberries commercially picked by transients in huckleberry plains in this area, particularly near Naples, Michigan, a small settlement east of Sharon which does not appear on present state maps. Naples, during the huckleberry season, was a town consisting of tents occupied by the berry pickers. The population was large enough to support several berry buyers and these people lived here only during the huckleberry season. They were really camping out, doing their cooking and washing at their tent homes and visiting in the evenings.

When the lumberjacks arrived in town on pay days their first stop was the grocery store where they stocked up on plug tobacco, smoking tobacco, new socks and other clothing they might need. They also bought delicacies they did not get in camp such as canned peaches and other fruit, which they took out to the sleighs, opened with knives, and ate outdoors with great relish. Then they headed for the saloons to drink, play cards, and have stag dances as there were no women available. These stag dances were boisterous affairs as the men wore their heavy calked boots, stomping and kicking and jigging to the music and really letting off steam after a month in the woods. As I remember it, the music was supplied by someone with an accordion and another man with a banjo. I do not recall what the tunes were to which they danced except that they were fast and noisy. I vaguely remember the words "Mary Ann McGee" and "down at Casey's dump" as fragments from some of these songs.

The dances were often broken up with fights, some of which were rough. I recall seeing one lumberjack stomp his calked boots across the face of another whom he had down

Above: Jacob Dye in a cutter (a sleigh for personal driving). He liked to own and drive good horses. When the horse really stepped out, you sometimes had to dodge packed ice from the flying hoofs.

Below: Road building as it was done in 1907.

on the floor. The face of the man who was stomped resembled fresh and bloody hamburger.

As the evening came to an end the heads of the various camps got their crews together, loaded them on bobsleighs, and headed back to their respective camps. The men who were too drunk to move under their own power were laid out on the blankets on the sleighs and would be ready to go back to work after they sobered up. They would, however, if they worked for my father, stay sober till the next pay day.

The only exception I can remember to this rule of my father's was a cook he had who would get well "oiled" between pay days on lemon extract. He must have been a very good cook as my father did not fire him but instead tried to keep him off the stuff. One day, however, the cook disappeared and my father later found him in the State Hospital for the Insane at Traverse City. Perhaps the lemon extract addiction finally caused such deterioration of brain cells as to destroy him.

In the summer, when working the cedar swamps was impossible, my father sometimes set up a tent store at Naples during the huckleberry season. He would supply quart boxes and berry crates for the pickers and buy berries from them for shipment to city markets. He also had a stock of supplies for sale to the pickers such as coffee, groceries, and tobacco.

Lumberjacks rarely smoked cigarettes although a few would roll their own, using Bull Durham or Prince Albert tobacco. Smoking was mostly pipe smoking with the corncob or briar pipe most in use. The tobacco used was mostly Five Brothers, Peerless, Giant, and Prince Albert as I recall it, and the first three of these brands were strong enough to ruin a pipe for most smokers today.

Most lumberjacks chewed tobacco such as Spearhead plug, Light and Dark Burley, which came in large round tins holding a pound, Mail Pouch and some "scrap" mixtures which were sweet and juicy.

Most of them took pride in being able to do a day's work, in their skill with the axe, saw, or other activity of the camps. They were paid about a dollar a day and board, as I recall it, the amount a bricklayer today would earn in about six minutes!

If they wanted to go anywhere they walked, except on pay days when they rode into town. An automobile was something you heard about but rarely saw. The first one I saw was in Traverse City much later. It was a steam powered vehicle and was having trouble keeping up enough steam to keep it in motion. I remember several boys and myself following it on foot around town.

In summer the cedar swamps were wet and filled with mosquitoes. They used to say that the mosquitoes were so big they could eat a man and then pick their teeth with a peavey. I can recall my brother and I exploring in these swamps, going from log to log with water a foot or more deep beneath the logs and fallen timber. Cedar lumbering was a winter activity insofar as woods working was concerned. Logs stockpiled at the mill, however, could be processed into ties, shingles, and net floats during the summer months.

My brother and I went to school at Sharon for several winters, walking about three miles from the camps. Once when we were going home from school, a big cat (bobcat or lynx) started following us. I told my brother to get well ahead of me and I had a solid club in my hand ready to use if necessary. The cat continued to follow us but as we neared the camp, it decided to leave and disappeared. We told our folks about it when we got home and my father and one of the men backtrailed us. They found big cat tracks but no cat. In the summer we went swimming in Cannon Creek and Devil's Creek, and went trout fishing with homemade tackle. We could always get enough brook trout for a good meal, using grasshoppers or angle worms for bait. Fishing was largely a matter of getting to the stream as the dense brush and undergrowth made it rough going. The water was very clear and very cold, ideal for brook trout.

During the winter we spent a great deal of time outdoors, even camping out with no tent. We would fall a small tree, trim it, and place it between two branches of larger trees. We would then trim some smaller poles and arrange them slanting from this "ridge pole" back to the ground, covering them with brush from the cedars to make a good shelter. We would then roll a log up in front of the open side of this shelter and use it as a backup for a fire which kept us warm and upon which we could fry bacon and speckled trout to make a meal.

I had one experience with yellow jackets I remember well. A yellow jacket is a particularly vicious type of bee that nests in the ground and will attack in swarms. I sat down on what appeared to be a small mound. It was a yellow jacket colony. They went after me, stung me, and chased me almost home.

When I told my father what had happened he got a long pole, wrapped one end of it with rags and tied them on. He then soaked the rags with kerosene and went back to the yellow jacket nest, lit the rags, and shoved the burning torch into it. That ended the yellow jacket problem.

While deer, bear, fox, and other wildlife were quite plentiful, there never was much hunting or trapping around the camps. Once in awhile someone would get a deer with his "30-30" Winchester or Marlin, but the meat was not particularly appetizing to the lumberjacks who would rather have had their baked beans and salt pork.

My father seemed never to have any fear of anything but spiders and snakes. I recall one camp we were in which was in an area infested with snakes. He solved the problem by buying a lot of hogs and turning them loose in the area. He later had the hogs slaughtered which provided a lot of fresh pork roasts and chops as well as plenty of salt pork for the crews. He also had a lot of this meat fried and packed in the lard rendered from the pork. It kept well and tasted like fried fresh pork when reheated for the table.

One experience that I remember vividly was a visit my father and I made to an old man who lived alone in a one-room log cabin. This man seemed very old to me at the time. He stood at the door with a rifle in his hand but when he saw who it was he asked us to come in. The thing that made a great impression on me was the fact that he had built shelving which covered one whole wall of this room, and on these shelves were cubbyholes filled with Edison cylinder records. He had an Edison phonograph with a big flower-shaped horn and played a lot of those records for us. I had never seen a phonograph before and to hear the music coming out of that horn was almost unbelievable at that time. Here, again, I do not know where we came from, or where we went afterward, but this experience is still with me. It probably happened about 1905 when I was six years old.

Now, in 1973, these memories of experiences, occurring well over a half century ago, seem remote and almost un-real. If one were to have said then that you would be able to turn a knob on a box smaller than an orange crate and see a live picture of such an event as the Watergate in-vestigation, or that men would travel to the moon, you would have been considered ready for the "booby hatch."

And perhaps, half a century from now our present way of life and technology will seem equally as primitive to our grandchildren and great-grandchildren. And I wonder if future generations will be as close to the realities of life and living as were those of a half century ago.